The Noahide Laws - God

Rechov Rabbi Akiva 164, Bnei Brak, Israel 03.616.6340
360 Valley Ave #23, Hammonton, N.J. 08037. 732.370.3344 fax 1.877.Pirchei

Table of Contents:

God

Introduction

This week's lesson will begin our parallel series of lessons on Noahide belief and thought. We will begin with where all things began: God.

God: The Transcendent and Immanent

God is easy and simple – utterly uncomplicated in any way.[1] However, our ability to comprehend Him is another matter. Anything we can say about God is more about how we perceive Him than about God himself. This is because God, as we shall see, is entirely transcendental. His essence is utterly beyond all comprehension. In fact, God is indescribable and ultimately unknowable.[2] However, God is also immanent and involved with His creation. From this feature of God we can learn a lot about Him, deriving His desires and values. This is perhaps the most famous example of God's essence versus our perception of God: although God is ultimately simple, we perceive Him as both transcendent and immanent. This idea is at the heart of much Torah theology and a good starting point for our discussion.

The Transcendent Aspect of God

The prayer Shema states: "Hear O Israel, The Lord our God, The Lord is one!" This declaration of God's unity is not merely about the mathematics of faith. It is more correctly understood as a qualitative rather than quantitative idea. God is

---

[1] See *Derech HaShem* I: 1. Although God is entirely simple and in no way possesses any plurality, we describe his influence upon creation using a variety of attributes (mercy, justice, love, etc.). These relate to our understanding, however, not to God's actual essence. See also *Ohr HaShem* I: 3:4; *Shnei Luchos HaBris* (in the Bris Dovid) I: 42; *Mishnah Torah Yesodei HaTorah* 2:10.

[2] *Shomer Emunim* 2:11. See also *Mishnah Torah Hil. Teshuva* 5:5 and *Emunos Ve-Deos* II.

not simply "one." Instead he is "oneness," the ultimate unity.[3] The problem with ultimate one-ness is that its nature precludes two-ness. For that matter, it precludes three-ness, four-ness, or anything-else-ness at all! If that is the case, then how do we exist? The answer is an important concept called *tzimtzum*: constriction. Before God could create anything at all, He had to create a space in which creation could take place. In order to do so, He "constricted" his presence, creating a space in which the essence of one-ness was diluted enough to allow creation to endure. This empty space is known as the *Chalal ha-Penui* (or *Chalal*, for short), the vacated space. Between God's eternal, unified essence and the *Chalal* a barrier called the *Pargod*, the veil, or partition.[4]

The *Chalal* is the canvas upon which all creation took place. Anything that is not-God exists as a created entity within the *Chalal*. As God Himself said: "I am God; I make all things."[5]

This distinct separation between God and His creation yields a number of conclusions about God:

- As creator of all things, God must therefore be, in essence, entirely separate from all things.[6] There is nothing in the created world that can represent or approximate Him. As it states in Isaiah: "To whom will you then liken God?"[7] Similarly: "There is none like you among the heavenly powers…"[8] Since God must be distinct from the creation, Judaism and Noahism must reject any concept of pantheism.

- Since God created all things, his existence can in no way be predicated upon anything in creation. We cannot therefore define God as love,

---

[3] See Rambam *13 Principles of Faith* and *Peirusha al HaMishnayos* Sanhedrin 10:1.

[4] This entire paragraph is a summary of the initial creation as explained by the Zohar and early mystics.

[5] Isaiah 44:24.

[6] *Shomer Emunim* 2:11.

[7] 40:18.

[8] Psalms 86:8.

morality, or any kind ethical force.[9] God may have those attributes, but they are not God and vice versa.[10]

- Since He created all matter, God must not be made of matter.[11] Similarly, since God created space and time, He cannot exist within space and time.[12]

What emerges from the above is a picture of a God who is entirely transcendent and beyond is creation. The danger of such a conception, however, is the erroneous conclusion that God is absent from His creation. To the contrary - God is intimately involved with His creation.

The Immanent Aspect of God

Tzimtzum does not mean that God totally removed Himself from the *Chalal*. It only means that he restricted his essence to a degree necessary for creation to endure.   Yet, God's presence still permeates and fills the *Chalal*.

How do we know this?

In Nechemiah 9:6 we are told:

You have made the heavens… the earth and all that is on it… you give life to them all.

The last clause is in the present tense: God gives life and is continuously giving life. There are many other references to God as the perpetual creator throughout the Tanakh.[13]

---

[9] *Pardes Rimonim* III: 1; *Yesodei HaTorah* 1:4; *Zohar* I: 22a.

[10] *Kuzari* II: 2; *Ikkarim* II: 22.

[11] See *Kuzari* 4:3. Because of His complete detachment from any element of the physical world he is called "pure" and "holy" in many places in Tanakh.

[12] *Emunos VeDeyos* II: 11 & 12 and Shvil *Emunah* ad loc.; *Ikkarim* II: 18; *Asara Maamaros Choker Din* I: 16. This is the Torah's answer to the famous paradox of free will vs. fore-knowledge. If God knows all things before they occur, then how do we have free will? The paradox arises from the assumption is that our choice is a result of God's fore –knowing. However, this cause and effect relationship only exists from our perspective. From God's perspective, in which time is irrelevant, cause does not precede nor follow effect. Our choice and God's knowledge have no temporal relationship to one-another and, therefore, there is no paradox.

Since creation's continued existence depends constantly upon God's will, then His will must extend into the *Chalal*. However, since God is an absolute unity, then his will and his essence must be one in the same. Therefore, God's essence must extend into the *Chalal*.

In this sense, God is immanent: He is continuously and intimately involved with His creation. He directs and sustains it, He hears and answers the prayers of His people; He gives it life and deals with it in kindness and justice. We see this on every page of the Tanakh.

The Experience of God vs. the Reality of God

We must be reminded, however, that this is a dual perception of God, and not relevant to God himself. It is a product of the finite mind's striking against an infinite reality. It is not a perception limited only to humans, however. This dual experience of God is alluded to in the song of the angels in Isaiah 6:3. The angels sing:

> *Holy, Holy, Holy us the God of hosts, the whole world is filled with his glory.*

This verse refers to the immanent experience of God. However, the angels also sing

> *Blessed is God's glory from His place.*[14]

Here the angels refer to God in the transcendental sense, as occupying a place that is His, only His, and that of none other.

Similarly, we say in the *Shema*: "Hear O Israel, the Lord our God, the Lord is one." Before declaring that God is an unknowable and transcendent unity ("the Lord is One"), we first declare that he is "the Lord our God," both imminent and ruling.

Furthermore, in every blessing we open with the words: *Blessed are you, our God, king of the universe.* We declare God as both *our God*, imminent and close, and as a king who is transcendent and lofty.

---

[13] Perpetual creation is fundamental and intrinsic to all Torah theology. See *Kuzari* 4:26; *Ibn Ezra Shemos* 3:2; *Ramban Bereshis* 1:4; *Yesodei HaTorah* 2:9; Zohar III:31a; *Pardes Rimonim* 6:8; *Reishis Chochmah Shaar HaYirah* I; there are too many sources to list here – this is only a sampling.

[14] Ezekiel 3:12.

The moving prayer *Ovinu Malkeinu*, recited several times during the year, repeats the refrain *Ovinu Malkeinu – Our father, our King!,* referring to God as both our imminent father and our transcendent king.

For Discussion   *In the live class we will discuss the following questions: if we know that God is the ultimately one, then why do we seem to focus this dual perception in our prayers and other sacred writings? For that matter, why do we speak of God as "angry" or "loving" if these are all only facets of our perception? Isn't there a better way to approach God?*

God's Incorporeality

As mentioned above, since God is the creator of all matter and all space, he cannot be made of matter or subject to space. This fact precludes God having any material manifestation. God himself warns us to never think of him corporeally, saying:

Take heed of yourselves for you saw no matter of form on that day that God spoke to you at Horeb...[15]

Nevertheless, the Torah often speaks of God using anthropomorphism – describing Him as if he had physical qualities. For example, in many places we find reference to the hand of God[16] or the eyes of God.[17] In all such situations the Torah is not telling us that God has a body. Rather, the Torah is borrowing from the language of man in order to express something about His relationship to His creation.[18]

Similarly, when the Torah describes God's voice, it is referring to a prophetic voice within the mind, but not to an actual divine voice in the sense that we understand voice.[19]

You wonder then why man is described as being created in God's image if God has no actual "image?"

____

[15] Deuteronomy 4:15.

[16] Exodus 9:15.

[17] Psalms 15:3.

[18] See *Ramban* to Genesis 46:1;

[19] *Kuzari* I: 89; *Emunos VeDeyos* 2:12.

This is not a description of the physical attributes of man – rather it means that man can affect and interact with the world using many of the same attributes perceived in God.[20] For example, Man and God both share free will and creative ability.

Other Issues

Any descriptor for God must be qualified and considered carefully. For example, God is often referred to as "He," in the masculine. However, this is merely an effect of the Hebrew language which has no neuter grammatical gender.

In the same vein, even terms that seem accurate must be kept in perspective. For example, God is often described as "eternal." As apropos as this may appear, it is still a limited description. Not being bound by time, the human concept of "eternity" doesn't even fit properly. "Eternal" is only the closest term we can use to describe God-in-time.

Overview

Although God is utterly beyond any description, comprehension, or corollary in the created universe, he is nevertheless intimately involved in it.

We see His impact upon reality at every turn, which informs us as to his will and attributes.

Nevertheless, these attributes are only products of our perception of God's action and not intrinsic to God Himself. We can only understand God's essence by knowing what it is not. In this sense, Torah theology is called "negative theology."

---

[20] *Nefesh HaChaim* I: 1; *Avodas HaKodesh, HaYichud* 18; *Mechilta Shemos* 14:29; *Hilchos Teshuva* 5:1.

Summary of the Lesson

1. God is beyond any words, description, form, or comprehension.

2. Since God created time, space, and matter, He is not subject to any of them.

3. Although God is entirely transcendent, he is also completely immanent and involved with the world.

4. This dual perception of God is only a perception and is not the reality of God. We are limited in our ability to perceive the infinite.

5. God is incorporeal and without form. Anthropomorphism is used by the Torah, however, to convey by way of allegory God's attributes in this world.

6. Any positive description of God is only a description of God's actions and influence, not of God himself. The essence of God can only be truly communicated by contemplating what God is not.

The Noahide Laws - Man

Rechov Rabbi Akiva 164, Bnei Brak, Israel 03.616.6340
360 Valley Ave #23, Hammonton, N.J. 08037. 732.370.3344 fax 1.877.Pirchei

Table of Contents:

Man, Reward, and Punishment

Introduction

In our last lesson on theology and belief we discussed the Torah conception of God. In this lesson we will explore man.

The Purpose of Creation

"Why did God create the world?" is perhaps the hardest question ever asked. To answer it, we have to presuppose an understanding of God's exact will and innermost thoughts before creation. If you studied the prior lesson on God carefully, then you will realize that this is impossible[1].

To further complicate things, consider that God is an absolute perfection, without lack or needs. He didn't need to create us. Therefore, his ultimate reasons for doing so are unfathomable.

Any discussion of God's purpose is only possible from our perspective as the beneficiary of creation.

The Greatest Act of Love

Taking into consideration all that we cannot know, it informs us as to what we do know. If G-d is perfect and had no need to create us, then the act of creation must

---

[1] See *Moreh Nevukhim* 3:13; Yoma 38a; *Avos d'Rabbi Nasan* 41.

stand as the ultimate act of altruism.[2] The Psalms speak of creation as such, describing it as an act of love:

The world is built of love.[3]

It is also an act of the ultimate goodness:

God saw all that He made and – behold! It was very good![4]

Since God is perpetually creating all reality,[5] it means that His goodness and love is constantly sustaining all creation:

God is good to all; His love is upon all his works.[6]

At every instant God's pure desire for us flows throughout every atom of creation.

Partaking of True Good

You let me know the path of life; in your presence is the fullness of joy. In your right hand is eternal bliss.[7]

I am The Lord your God who instructs you for your own reward…[8]

---

[2] *Emunos VeDeos* I:4; *Reshis Chochma Shaar HaTeshuva* I; *Derech HaShem* I:2:1; *Sheni Luchos HaBris, Beis Yisroel* I:21b; *Likutei Moharan* 64.

[3] 89:3.

[4] Genesis 1:35.

[5] This is the doctrine of perpetual creation discussed in an earlier lesson.

[6] Psalms 145:9.

[7] Psalms 16:11.

[8] Isaiah 48:17.

This first verse tells us that God is the ultimate goodness[9]. The second verse tells us both that Man is capable of partaking of that ultimate goodness and that God instructs us as to how we should do so.[10]

However, in order to be aware of divine goodness, we must know its absence. This is another reason for *tzimtzum*, the restriction of God's presence in the physical creation.[11] By reducing the everyday immanent experience of God, true experiences of His goodness can be fully recognized.

Free Will

I call heaven and earth to witness against you this day: I have put before you life and death, blessing and curse. Choose life…[12]

This verse alludes to man's free will – his ability to choose whether to partake of God's goodness or to turn away from it.

If man had no free will, then enjoyment of God's goodness would not be true enjoyment. It would be a compulsory, rote experience devoid of greater meaning. Once he has the ability to desire and choose God's goodness, only then does the experience becomes valuable.[13]

Therefore, God created man with free will. Besides God, man is the only being who can act upon his free choice. In this sense, man resembles God. This is the fundamental understanding of man having been created "in the image of God."[14]

Free will, however, requires both an internal and external mechanism in order to function.

---

[9] *Ibn Ezra ad* loc; *Emunos VeDeyos* III. See also *Derech HaShem* I:2:1.

[10] *Emunos VeDeos* I:4.

[11] See the lesson on God.

[12] Deuteronomy 30:19.

[13] There is a massive amount of literature on the necessity of free will. For a basic overview, see *Hilchos Teshuva* 5; *Emunos VeDeyos* IV:4; *Reishis Chochmah Shaar Teshuva* I; Zohar I:23a.

[14] See *Derech HaShem* I:2.

Internal Aspects: Yetzer Tov vs. Yetzer Hara	Internally, man is imbued with two opposing forces:

- The *yetzer tov* – the desire for good, altruism, self-betterment, and mitzvos.
- The *yetzer hara* – the desire for evil, selfishness, self-destruction, and transgression.

This dual nature of man explains the apparent contradiction between these two verses:

> *And God created man in his image; in the image of G-d he created him.*[15]
>
> and
>
> *The desire of man's heart is evil from his youth.*[16]

The first verse refers to man's divine potential – the *yetzer tov*, the desire for good. The second refers to man's base desires – his *yetzer hara*, the desire for evil.

In the Talmud,[17] Rabbi Nachman bar Rav Chisda sees an allusion to both aspects in the verse

> *And God formed [רמ"צ] man…*

Rabbi Nachman points out that the word רמ"צ is spelled with and extra yud. He sees the two yuds in the word as an allusion to God's having formed man with two desires (also, the word *yotzer*, formed, is a cognate of the word *yetzer*, desire).

In Torah thought all of man's actions and choices are the result of a struggle between these two inclinations. One seeks the holy, the other the profane - one desires knowledge, the other wants only physical pleasure.

One might think that the goal of man is to entirely ignore his evil desire. This is not so. The ideal for man is to subdue his bad desire to his good desire, thus making it a tool of divine service.

---

[15] Genesis 1:27.

[16] Genesis 8:21.

[17] *Berachos* 61a.

External Aspects: Man vs. the World

In order for Man to have free will, he must be placed in an environment that allows him to exercise his power of choice. Therefore, God created a world filled with opportunities for both good and evil in which all things speak to his ultimate purpose:

God has made everything for his own purpose, even the wicked…[18]

I form light and create darkness. I make peace and create evil. I am God – I do all these things.[19]

In this environment, any and every decision a person makes is the direct result of a nuanced struggle between these opposite inclinations.

How man decides to use or pervert the opportunities God offers is man's choice alone and one for which he bears 100% of the responsibility:

If a person sins… he bears full responsibility for his action.[20]

Since the potential for evil resides within man and is evenly matched with his capacity for good, the Torah rejects any concept of an all-evil being or devil who temps people into sin. To iterate: people are 100% responsible for their own sins.

Reward & Punishment

We tend to think that we are rewarded *for* our good deeds and punished *for* our transgressions. This view is true only of laws created and administered by man. Spiritual reward and punishment operate according to a different mechanic. Just as God created the natural world with its own principles of cause and effect, He did the

---

[18] Proverbs 16:4.

[19] Isaiah 45:7.

[20] Leviticus 5:17.

same with the spiritual world.[21] Within this system reward and punishment are *direst results* of one's actions rather than things meted out *for* one's actions.[22]

This idea runs throughout *Tanakh:*[23]

A wicked man's sins shall entrap him; he will be bound in the binds of his own transgression.[24]

God is known by the judgment he carries out when the wicked man is ensnared in the work of his own hands.[25]

He who digs a pit shall fall into it.[26]

These two verses make clear that God's justice is programmed into the spiritual law of the universe and operates as a direct result of one's own actions. The same applies to reward.[27] However, there is a difference: while punishment is precisely meted out, reward is given liberally.[28] Furthermore, the ultimate reward for good lasts for eternity while the punishment for evil is only temporary. Because the nature of reward and punishment differ, good deeds cannot cancel out evil and vice versa. This is learned from a verse in the Torah:

---

[21] Just as with His natural law, it is only altered in very rare circumstances. See *Shemos Rabbah* 30:6; *Vayikra Rabbah* 35:3; *Yerushalmi Rosh HaShanah* 1:3.

[22] Numerous Midrashim discuss this idea. *See Koheles Rabbah* 3:11; *Vayikra Rabbah* 19:6; *Yalkut Shimoni* 2:938.

[23] For more examples see Proverbs 13:6; Obadiah 1:15; Psalms 18:25-26.

[24] Proverbs 5:22

[25] Psalms 9:17.

[26] Proverbs 6:27.

[27] *Sotah* 1:8; *Tosefta Sotah* 4:1; *Bava Metzia* 86a; *Sotah* 17a; *Chullin* 89a; *Sefer Chassidim* 53. There are many, many, sources and examples.

[28] See *Sotah* 9b; *Sefer Chasidim* 698; *Tos. Yom Tov* on Sotah 9:8; *Tos. Sotah* 11a s.v. Miriam. Again, there are many, many, sources and examples.

God does not give special consideration or take bribes.[29]

What does it mean that God does not take bribes? Our sages explain that God does not take the exchange of good deeds for evil ones.[30]

An individual is punished for all the evil he does and rewarded for all of the good.

However, the punishment that one deserves for his transgressions can be changed into the merit of a mitzvah by sincere, loving repentance.[31]

Reward in This World?

As we will see in a future lesson, the primary place for reward and punishment is *Olam Haba*, the World to Come. Nevertheless, under certain circumstances, a person can receive reward and punishment for part of his deeds in this world. We will discuss this more in future lessons.

Middah Keneged Middah

Many times, but not always, there is an obvious correspondence between the deed and its reward and the crime and its punishment. This relationship is called *middah keneged middah – measure-matching-measure*. When this happens it is in order to demonstrate God's law and further reveal his kingship in the world.[32]

---

[29] Deuteronomy 10:17.

[30] See Ramban ad loc.; Avos 4:22 and numerous commentaries ad. loc.;

[31] *Yoma* 86a; *Yerushalmi Peah* 1:1; *Ikkarim* 4:25; *Shemos Rabbah* 31:1; *Bamidbar Rabbah* 10:1; *Shir HaShirim Rabbah* 6:1 and much more.

[32] See *Ikkarim* IV: 9; *Mekhilta Shemos* 14:26 and 18:11; *Shabbos* 105b; *Sanhedrin* 90a; *Nedarim* 32a and many, many more examples.

Summary of the Lesson

1. God's innermost reasons for wanting to create the world are mysterious and cannot be understood. We can only understand His reasons from our perspective as the beneficiaries of creation.

2. Creation was the greatest, truest, and purest act of love and altruism. Since God is constantly creating, His love and goodness are constantly being sustaining the world.

3. It is possible for man to partake of and experience the underlying goodness that sustains creation. He does so by keeping the mitzvos and serving and clinging to God.

4. In order to know this good, we much know its absence. This is another reason for the idea of *tzimtzum*.

5. Man must voluntarily earn this good; otherwise his benefit would not be true benefit. Only by choosing it voluntarily does man truly enjoy it. Therefore God gave man free will.

6. In this aspect of free will man, in a very small way, resembles his Creator. This is the idea of man having been made in God's image.

7. To enable free will, man was given two conflicting internal drives: a desire to do good and a desire to do bad. Man was also placed in an environment which provides him with choices and contexts in which to exercise his will.

8. Reward and punishments are best conceived as the effects of our choices rather than judgments that are meted out. Reward and punishment are the effects of a "spiritual law" established by God and similar to natural law.

9. One's mitzvos cannot cancel out his transgressions. A person is rewarded for all of his mitzvos and punished for all of his sins. However, sincere repentance can convert ones sins into merits.

10. The primary place for reward and punishment is not in this world. Nevertheless, some reward and punishment is possible in this world depending on the circumstances.

11. Occasionally the relationship between the mitzvah/reward and the sin/punishment is obvious. Sometimes it is not.

The Noahide Laws – The Soul

164 Village Path, Lakewood NJ 08701 732.370.3344
164 Rabbi Akiva, Bnei Brak, 03.616.6340

Table of Contents:

The Soul

The Material Body & the Immaterial Soul

God formed man out of the dust of the ground and breathed into his nostrils a breath of life. Man then became a living being.[1]

This famous verse describes man as a being created of two natures: the physical (the dust of the ground) and the spiritual (the soul – the breath of life). A subtle nuance of this verse is that man was animated with God's breath – an exhalation from the innermost being of God. This is in contrast to the rest of creation, which was created by G-d's speech – with sound waves created by God – which is a lower level of divine intimacy, one that is distanced from God's essence.[2]

Of course,

> God does not actually have breath. This is a merely a descriptive metaphor enabling us to discuss the concepts involved. It is an extremely apt one, however, and is elaborated upon greatly by our Sages.

The Glassblower[3]

The parable used by many sages to describe the nature of the soul is that of a glassblower creating a vessel. The glassblower dips one end of his tube into molten glass and places the other end against his lips. The breath originates at the lips, flows down the tube, and comes to rest in the molten glass below, forming it and shaping it into its final form as the glass blower rotates and turns the whole apparatus. Now, where is the soul in this analogy? Is it upon the lips of the glass blower, in the tube, or in the burgeoning glass bulb at the end? The answer is all three.

---

[1] Genesis 2:7

[2] See *Likutey Amazim, Sefer Shel Beinonim II; Nefesh HaChaim 11:15.*

[3] See the *Derech HaShem* of Rabbi Moshe Chaim Luzzatto (1707 – 1746).

The Three Expressions of the Soul[4]

The soul is constantly being "blown" into the being by God. As such, the soul exists in a constant dynamic relationship with its creator. This ongoing emanation of the soul means that the soul constantly exists in three expressions. Many writers have described these three expressions as levels, or components of the soul. However, such descriptions are misleading. I prefer to call it three "expressions" of the soul:

1) **Neshamah**, meaning "soul," and derived from the word *Neshima*, meaning "breath." In our parable, this is the exit of the breath from the lips of the divine glassblower. This is the essence of the soul and its highest and most intimate connection to God.

2) **Ruach**, meaning "spirit," and derived from the word for wind. This is the moving, blowing of the soul into the world, representing the raging conduit and connection between man's soul and God.

3) **Nefesh**, often translated as "soul," yet better translated as "life-force," is from the word *Nafash*, meaning "to rest." It alludes to the divine breath coming to rest in the vessel of the body of man.

These three expressions exist simultaneously and in constant interaction with each other. While the *Neshama* is the closest to God and the place at which the soul's truest essence resides, it is bound to the *Nefesh*, the component that enlivens the body and interacts with the rest of creation, via *Ruach*, the conduit of divine breath.

These soul-elements form a chain binding man's soul to G-d:

The Nefesh is bound to the *Ruach, the* Ruach is bound to the *Neshama, and the* Neshama to the Holy One, Blessed is He.[5]

The Five Expressions of the Soul

The Midrash,[6] however, adds two more levels to the soul:

---

[4] Based upon the *Nefesh HaChaim* of Rabbi Chaim Vital.

[5] Zohar 3:25a.

1) *Chayah*, "living essence," and,

2) *Yechidah*, "unique essence."

Our scholars understand these as two higher, almost completely imperceptible levels of the soul. They are, like God Himself, both immanent and transcendent in relationship to the lower levels of the soul.

If the *Neshama* is the breath of God, the glassblower, then *Chayah* is the body of the glassblower, the vehicle which gives motion to and exhales the divine breath. Note, though, that the breath exhaled by the glassblower is not intrinsic to His being.

Therefore,

> The lower levels of the soul originate from His "body," so to speak, yet are not "of" his body; they are a separate, created entity independent of, yet intimately originating from, the creator.

Yechidah, however, is something totally transcendent. It represents the true, inexpressible aspect of the creator. It is the innermost part of the creator which desires to create and knows its own purposes. In our parable, *Yechidah* is the soul of the glassblower, the innermost essence of God.

Man can only access the three lower levels of the soul: *Neshama*, *Ruach*, and *Nefesh*. The upper two levels belong to God Himself.

The Expressions of the Soul in This World

Each expression of the soul exerts its own influence over particular areas of human activity.

Nefesh, the lowest level, governs man's physical interaction with the world. It transfers will into the animation of the body. It also binds the rest of the soul to the physical matter of the body.

Ruach, the motion of the divine spirit, is the source of the power of speech. It is responsible for the articulation and organization of inspiration into thought. This power, combined with *Ruach's* duty as the conduit between the lower and higher

---

[6] See Midrash Koheles Rabbah to Koheles 3:21 and Bereshis Rabbah 14:9.

expressions of the soul, also makes it the conduit for divine inspiration. Divine inspiration, in Hebrew, is called *Ruach ha-kodesh*, or holy *Ruach*. Ruach is also the realm of the emotions.

Neshama influences the higher realm of human faculties such as thought, intellect, and the spiritual sensibilities.

The Lower Soul

We tend to think of the soul as a purely spiritual entity, which it is. However, what about animals? Do they have souls? The answer is "yes." However, their souls are not spiritual. Instead, they are the most ethereal of physical entities.[7]

What is more, all living beings possess this *nefes ha-behamis* – this "animal soul." This includes man as well.[8] This animal soul is the most basic force needed to maintain life. It is the animating force that governs the "natural laws" of physiology and most basic needs for survival.

This soul is what the Torah refers to when it states:

The soul of the flesh that is in the blood.[9]

This animal soul is essential for guaranteeing the survival of the organism. Without it, the spiritual soul would never eat, engage in reproduction, or do anything other than pray and pursue connection to God. This physical soul is what is also known as the *yetzer hora*, the evil desire discussed in earlier lessons.[10]

---

[7] See *Derech HaShem* on the soul.

[8] Eitz Chaim 49:3; Derech HaShem III: 1:1; Zohar II: 94b; Ramban to Genesis 1:20, Leviticus 17:14, and many, many more sources.

[9] Leviticus 17:11; Targum ad loc.

[10] Brachos 5a, 54a, 60b, 61b; Sanhedrin 91b; Derech HaShem I: 3:1 and II: 2:2.

The Immortality of the Soul

All souls that will ever exist were created at the beginning of time. Since then they have been kept in a celestial repository until God deems them to be born.[11] Upon death, the soul ascends to a new place, the *olam ha-neshamos*, where it resides until the coming of the messiah. However, it doesn't always work out this way.

Gilgul HaNeshomos – Reincarnation[12]

Reincarnation, though subject to some debate in the past[13], is an accepted part of Torah belief.[14] However, reincarnation is a loaded term with lots of non-Torah connotations. We must, therefore, be cautious not to assume anything about the Torah's doctrine lest we color our understanding with the convoluted perversions of pop-culture.

In the Torah's view, reincarnation is neither an automatic nor a common event. It is also neither a punishment nor a reward. Instead, reincarnation is an act of divine compassion. God gives many *neshamos,* souls, a "second chance" to fulfill mitzvos that they may have missed in a previous life. This is sometimes needed to allow particular souls to accomplish unique *tikkunim*, repairs to the world, for which those souls are uniquely suited.

---

[11] Niddah 13b; Chagigah 12b; Eitz Chaim 26:2. There is some disagreement between the Kabbalists and rational philosophers over this detail. See Emunos VeDeos 6:3.

[12] This entire section is a summary of *Shaar Gilgul HaNeshamos* from the *Kisvei HaAri*.

[13] Even though the concept predated them, reincarnation was rejected strongly by Rav Saadia Gaon, R' Yosef Albo, and Raavad I (not to be confused with Raavad II, the Rambam's famous disputant). However, Rav Hai Gaon argued with Rav Saadia in defense of reincarnation. In the medieval era, it was upheld by the Ramban and Rabbeinu Bachya ben Asher. Throughout the renaissance it gained further scholarly attention and support.

[14] The Ari and Ramak's systematization of kabbalah provided a full theological defense and context for reincarnation. Their study let to its acceptance by both the Baal Shem Tov and the Vilna Gaon.

However, *neshamos*, souls, are not always reincarnated in whole or in the same form held in their previous life. Sometimes only some of the components of the soul (*Nefesh*, *Ruach*, or *Neshamah*) are reincarnated, carved away from their fellows. The reincarnated souls, or parts of souls, may also not come back in human form.

Reincarnation is not common, and full reincarnation in human form is exceptionally rare. However, it does happen. Noahides are subject to the doctrine of *Gilgul ha-neshamos*, reincarnation as are Jews.

Summary of This Lesson

1. Man was created with a physical being and a spiritual soul. The imbuing of the spiritual soul was a more intimate act of creation than the creation of the physical body. The body was created by speech, the soul by breath.

2. The soul is a single entity which emanates into the world, radiating as three distinct expressions. These expressions are a chain which binds the soul in this world to its origin.

3. Each expression influences particular human qualities.

4. There are higher expressions of the soul, but these are rooted in the being of God Himself and essentially unknowable to us.

5. Man, as all living creatures also has a natural, animal soul, which animates the basic, rote physiological processes and desires needed for survival. This soul is the root of the *yetzer hora*, the evil desire.

6. The soul is immortal. All souls were created at the beginning of creation and set aside by God until their time to be born. When a person dies, their soul is transferred to another repository to await the World to Come.

7. Some souls or portions of souls are reincarnated as an act of divine compassion. They are not always reincarnated in human form, however.

The Noahide Laws - Afterlife

164 Village Path, Lakewood NJ 08701 732.370.3344
164 Rabbi Akiva, Bnei Brak, 03.616.6340

Table of Contents:

The Afterlife, Messiah, and Redemption

Introduction

As we learned a few lessons ago, both Judaism and Noahism believe in the immortality of the soul. Naturally, this entails belief in an afterlife. Yet, there is a very sharp distinction between the western, Christianized view of the afterlife and the Torah's view.

Keeping Perspective

Compared to other belief systems, Judaism and Noahism focus very little on the afterlife. The afterlife is a particular pre-occupation of Christianity and Islam and an obsession that establishes the afterlife as the ultimate goal of all worldly activity. However, Torah references to the afterlife are almost non-existent. In fact, discussion of the afterlife is almost taboo and distasteful in many circles.

Many authors note this ongoing de-emphasis of the afterlife in Torah thought, connecting it to the exodus from Egypt. Egypt was a society obsessed with the afterworld to the point of corruption. Their afterlife was more real, immediate, and relevant than anything of this world.

Part of God's plan in taking the Jews out of Egypt was to cleanse them of this undue focus and set their priorities straight. God wants us to fulfill His will in <u>this</u> world – that is the purpose of creation. Therefore, the Torah is conspicuously devoid of any mention of the afterlife. The little we know about the afterlife and the World-to-Come is from scant references in the prophets, writings, and Oral Torah.

What is more, the rabbinic world has followed this trend, placing all of its emphasis on defining the fulfillment of God's will in this world. The study of the afterlife has remained a "fuzzy" topic for scholars.

While we know the general principles and order of things, the specific details are unclear. We must recall that no one has ever seen the afterlife. What we know about it we believe to be true with absolute faith. However, we must also have the humility to admit that which we do not know.

Taking this fact into account, scholars have realized that attempting to pin down a precise vision of the afterlife is not only impossible, but ultimately not a good a use of their time.

"Heaven" and "Hell?"

Judaism and Noahism do not believe in heaven and hell. The idea of eternal damnation and suffering without relief just doesn't work. Consider that we believe God punishes commensurate with deeds. Eternal punishment isn't commensurate with anyone's deeds because no one, now, never, or ever, is infinitely evil or has committed an infinite number of evil deeds.

Another problem with hell is that God's purpose for creating the world was the bestowal of good. Let's imagine that a theoretically infinitely-evil person exists and does get sent to hell for all eternity. Now, if God's purpose is good, yet this person will receive none if it ever again, then why does this evil person continue to exist at all? Is it that God is sadistic and wants to make our evil person suffer forever? It is possible to argue that eternal suffering exists as a deterrent from transgression. However, this is not a compelling argument; there are better ways to discourage sin.

The concept of Heaven is equally perplexing. A place where everyone gets the same reward regardless of their deeds?

Also, where do heaven and hell leave the early realm? In this paradigm of the afterlife, this world is has little purpose; the emphasis is entirely on the future life.

Christianity, well aware of these problems, has wrestled with them for centuries. Rather than coming to compelling consensus, their doctrine has become highly fragmented. This fracturing of belief is the source of many doctrinal disputes and widely differing eschatologies.

Judaism and Noahism, on the other hand don't suffer from this doctrinal schizophrenia because we have a very different vision of the afterlife.

Gan Eden

The following description of the afterlife and future worlds are summarized from Gesher HaChayim, The Bridge of Life, *by Rabbi Yechiel Michel Tukachinsky,* Derech HaShem, The Way of God, *by Rabbi Moshe Chaim Luzzatto, and* An Essay on Fundamentals, *also by Rabbi*

Luzzatto. This presentation is a general overview of the beliefs, yet is nothing here is an iron-clad fundamental-of-the-faith.

God prepared a number of places for the soul. In this physical world at this time, the place of the soul is the body. However, when the body is no longer available, God prepared another repository: *Gan Eden*, the Garden of Eden. The Garden has an upper garden and a lower garden.

The Lower Garden

While both gardens are entirely spiritual, the lower one is a "shadow," a spiritual simulacrum of the physical world. In this lower realm the souls maintain an image of their physical form. Similarly, the delights of this lower realm are limited, experienced much as greatest pleasures of the physical world.

The Upper Garden

The upper garden, however, is a place where souls exist in their abstract, truest essence; they do not maintain the "shadow" of their physical form. Likewise, the delights of this upper garden are abstract and uniquely spiritual, devoid of corollary in the physical world.

The Gardens are not static. They experiences "seasons" and a spiritual "time" all of its own. Its delights, the fruits of the garden, change regularly with the seasons.

Shoel / Chibbut HaKever

However, the ability to enter these spiritual gardens necessitates the soul's detachment from the physical realm. The committing of transgressions has the effect of binding and entangling the soul with the physical world. In order for the soul to ascend, it must be carefully dis-entangled from *olam ha-zeh*, material existence.

Recall from our previous lesson on reward and punishment that punishment is not a "punishment for" as much as a "natural consequence of" sin.

We can now understand what this means. The "punishment" of sin is the disentanglement of the soul from the body. By nature, this is an unpleasant process, like disentangling a cotton ball from a thorn bush. The greater the transgressions, the more entangled the soul the longer and more unpleasant the experience.

Burial and Decomposition

This process begins with burial and the process of decomposition. Upon placement of the body in the grave (*shoel*), the "physical trap" of the soul returns to its source, losing its form and illusory autonomy. For approximately 12 months the soul hovers above the grave "grieving" and "mourning" for the loss of the body. This is the implication of the verses:

His soul mourns for him,[1]

and,

His flesh grieves for him.[2]

This process, called *chibbut ha-kever,* the atonement/purification of the grave, is of tremendous anguish to the soul.

Gehinnom

Once the soul has completed this *chibbut kever,* purification of the grave, it is then judged. At this point, the soul stands before the ultimate truth and must confront all of its deeds. This part of the afterlife is known as *Gehinnom.*

Since this is a purely spiritual process, it cannot be adequately described in words. Nevertheless, the Talmud, Midrash, and other sources attempt to convey the experience of the soul using graphic, often terrifying parables. For example, the description of *Gehenom* as a place of fire refers to the shame the soul experience as it stands before the ultimate truth.

The process of *Gehenom* is by not a permanent one; it lasts, at most, for only 12 months. After this point, the soul may ascend to the gardens.

Olam HaBa

Gan Eden, the Garden, *Gehinnom* – all of these places are temporary. The permanent place of man's reward is the World to Come, *Olam HaBa.* This future era, ushered in by the coming of the Messiah and resurrection of the dead (topics of future lessons), is one of the most mysterious and least-understood of God's creations.

Although the World to Come is a creation of G-d, no two souls experience it the same way. Rabbi Chaim of Volozhin, in his *Nefesh HaChayim* describes the unique experience of the world to come as follows:

---

[1] Job 14:22. See Shabbos 152a.

[2] Ibid.

A person's own deeds constitute his reward in the World to Come. Once the soul has departed the body, it arises to take pleasure and satisfaction in the power and light of the holy worlds that have been created and multiplied by his good deeds. This is what the Sages meant when they said: "All of Israel have a portion <u>to</u> the World to Come," and not <u>in</u> the World-to-Come. <u>In</u> implies that the World to Come is prepared and awaiting a person from the time of Creation, as if it was something existing on its own and of which man may receive as a reward. In truth, the World to Come is built of the expansion and multiplication of ones deeds into a place for himself… so too with the punishment of Gehenom, the sin itself is his punishment.

The structure and space of the world to come is directly related to the mitzvos of an individual. Within that space, the eternal reward of his *mitzvos* is received. The amount of reward, however, is directly tied to the merit one accumulated in this world.

There is a lack of clarity and agreement as to whether the World to Come is physical or entirely spiritual. There is also confusion as to the various roles within that world, the nature of *mitzvos*, and the purpose of worship, holidays, and the third temple.

In truth, though, these details are not entirely for us to know, but to find out eventually.

For those wanting to read more, see the *Bridge of Life* by Rabbi Yechiel Michel Tukachinsky (published by Moznaim) and the *Way of God* by Rabbi Moshe Chaim Luzzatto (published by Feldheim).

Summary of the Lesson

1. Upon death and burial, the process of decay begins. This atonement for the physical flesh via the grave is called *shoel*, literally, the grave.

2. As the soul decomposes, the soul undergoes a process of disentanglement from the body. This is known as *chibbut ha-kever*, the atonement/purification of the grave.

3. Following *chibbut ha-kever*, the soul then undergoes the first of a series of judgments. This is called *Gehenom*.

4. *Gehinnom* is the laying bare of one's sins in the light of complete truth. The many metaphors for *Gehinnom* found in the sources speak primarily to the emotional experience of *Gehinnom*.

5. The entire process of *Shoel*, *chibbut ha-kever*, and *Gehinnom*, takes 12 months at most.

6. Once the soul has been judged and is freed from its attachments to the physical, it ascends to *Gan Eden*, the Garden of Eden.

7. The Garden contains upper and lower gardens for different souls of different natures.

8. The Gardens experience seasons, fruits, and all the other varieties to be expected in a physical garden. Of course, these are all allegories for a non-physical place.

9. The soul awaits in the Gardens until the coming of the messiah. At this time the souls are reborn, experiencing resurrection.

10. The resurrection and rebirth is into a new world called *Olam Haba* – the world to Come.

11. The World to Come is a not well understood; it is also experienced differently by each soul commensurate with the *mitzvos* of that soul during its first lifetime.

The Noahide Laws – The Supernatural

Rechov Rabbi Akiva 164, Bnei Brak, Israel 03.616.6340
360 Valley Ave #23, Hammonton, N.J. 08037. 732.370.3344 fax 1.877.Pirchei

Table of Contents:

The Supernatural

Introduction

HaShem's creation is amazing and diverse, including far more than our physical senses allow us to perceive. The parts of creation lying beyond the senses are usually, and often erroneously, called "supernatural." However, these "supernatural" elements are actually far more natural than they may seem. They are part of the world and, in a sense, almost commonplace. Once we accept the paranormal as normal, the question of natural vs. unnatural becomes one of what constitutes natural vs. unnatural relationships to these entities. Most of the material cited here is summarized from the *Sefer HaBris*, *Derech HaShem*, and the writings of the Ari Zt"l. Know that this is a big topic – we will only give the scantest overview here.

Supernatural vs. Natural

It is a common mistake to assume that the sages made no distinction between natural and supernatural causation. For example, while many ancient peoples attributed disease to demons and spirits, the sages had a far more advanced understanding. There Talmud provides us with many examples:

- Kesubos 110b – The Talmud acknowledges that moving and other stressful life-changes might cause digestive problems.

- Taanis 21b – Rabbi Yehudah decreed a fast due to an epidemic among pigs. The Talmud asked: "Does Rabbi Yehudah hold that an epidemic of one species will spread to another?" The answer is surprising: "No, but the biology of pigs and humans is similar enough that they are likely to suffer from the same diseases."

- Bava Metzia 107b – Chills and colds are the result of wind; one did not bundle up sufficiently against the cold.

- And many, many, more…[1]

The Talmudic understanding is that there are unseen, yet natural causes for disease and other phenomena while, concurrently, there are also metaphysical and spiritual causes. It is very important to realize that, unlike many ancient peoples, the Sages did not simply attribute supernatural agency to events for which they lacked scientific or natural explanations.[2]

Ghosts

The soul's existence is entirely independent of the physical. However, the soul's ability to affect and benefit from this world is dependent on its remaining bound to the body. When the body ceases its biological function, the soul's existence continues, unhindered, upon its own plane. At that point, it has four options: it can either ascend to the gardens (as discussed previously), become reincarnated, seek refuge in another body (possession), or continue disembodied. The disembodied existence of an unclothed soul is only possible for a brief period of time. During this period the disembodied soul is not visible, yet can be sensed by the higher faculties of another soul.[3] Animals in particular are sensitive to such things and often sense them with greater ease than people.[4]

Apparitions

Apparitions are the auditory and/or visible manifestation of a soul that is no longer carried by a body. The most famous example of an apparition is from I

---

[1] Kesuvos 20a, 77a; Brachos 25a; Bava Kamma 60b; Sanhedrin 9a. There are many more sources.

[2] This isn't to imply that the sages always understood the scientific causation of things. After all, there are many examples of apparent scientific error in the Talmud. The most famous are Shabbos 107b, Pesachim 94b, and Chullin 127a. The Rambam famously wrote (*Moreh Nevuchim* 3:14) that the Sages relied upon the best science of their time, which was not always correct. There is significant dispute and debate as to how to understand these apparent errors and to what degree they impact religious practice. The important point is that the sages understood that there were phenomena whose exact causes, though invisible, were not by default supernatural. By the same token, they also understood there to be events of apparently natural mechanism whose roots were entirely supernatural. The result is a complicated world-view of subtle interplay between the physical causes of the spiritual and vice-versa.

[3] Megillah 3a – "Though he does not see, his *mazal* sees…"

[4] See Bava Kamma 60b and Maharal *Beer HaGolah* V, p. 98.

Samuel 28, in which King Saul used a necromancer to summon the soul of the prophet Samuel. A close reading of this event reveals that, while the necromancer was able to see the prophet, only Saul was able to converse with it. Similarly, Saul was able to communicate with Samuel, but could not see him. Ralbag[5] explains that only the necromancer was able to see Samuel because her imagination was focused on the visual appearance of Samuel. Saul, however, needed information from Samuel and, therefore, focused his mind on the conversation alone. This implies that the apparitions of the voice and appearance of the prophet did not exist physically. Instead, they were only projected into the minds of those attuned to perceiving them.

This is true of all apparitions, be they of spirits or angels. Daniel 10 buttresses this understanding:

I lifted up my eyes and looked and beheld a man clothed in linen… And I Daniel alone saw the vision, for the men that were with me saw it not; nevertheless, a great trembling took hold of them, and they fled…

Daniel alone perceived a form for the entity, while the others only sensed its presence. In truth, the entity had no form for it was an entirely spiritual presence.

Maimonides, in his *Hilchos Yesodei HaTorah*, writes:

One can never see matter without form or form without matter… The forms that are devoid of matter cannot be perceived with the physical eye, but only with the mind's eye.[6]

In every recorded instance of an apparition it required the presence of an observer.

It should be noted, that the conjuring of an apparition from the souls of the dead is a sever prohibition.

Angels

God cannot breach the veil between his essence and *Chalal* — the void in which all creation came to be. Were God's essence to intrude into this arena, all creation would immediately cease to be. The reason is that in the presence of God's

---

[5] Rabbi Levi ben Gershom (1288 – 1344). One of the great medieval bible commentators, a noted physician, and astronomer.

[6] 4:7.

absolute oneness, no other existence is possible. Therefore, to act directly upon this world, God needs an agent, a tool. These are the *Melakhim*, angels. They are mechanistic beings which exist to execute specific aspects of God's will upon the created world. The name of an angel alludes to its purpose:

- *Raphael* – From the words *rofe*, healer of, *Eyl*, God. This angel is the Healer of God, the one who brings healing to those who need it.

- *Gavriel* – From *gibor*, the mighty one, *ayl*, of God. This angel, the Mighty One of God, carries out acts of power and destruction.

- *Uriel* – From *Ohr*, light of, *Eyl*, God. The Light of God is the angel who illuminated, interprets, and explains.

- *Someil* – This angel, <u>whose name we never say</u>, is the Poison of God. His duty is to prosecute the wicked and execute God's punishment. He is sometimes called the *Soton* – the adversary.

Angels have no will independent of God's will. As purely spiritual beings, they have no physical appearance or shape. Instead, they exist as abstract forms. What then, are we to make of the many descriptions of angels found in the Tanakh?

Writes Maimonides:

> *...For the angels have no physical bodies, only abstract forms. What then is meant when the prophets report having seen a being of fire or with wings? These descriptions are part of the prophetic vision and should be understood allegorically.[7]*

We see that the vision and appearance of the angel, as experienced in the mind of the prophet, is part of the prophetic experience and part of the prophetic message.

Dybbuk & Gilgul

When a disembodied soul can no longer endure the limbo of being out-of-body, it may seek refuge in a living body currently inhabited by a soul. This is called a *Dybbuk*, a clinging spirit. There are many types of *Dybbuk im*, the most common of which is a *Dybbuk ibur*. This spirit clings to another body silently and has no influence or effect on the host. It merely rides along until the host achieves a certain condition spiritually that is of benefit to the *dybbuk*. Keep in mind,

---

[7] *Hilchos Yesodei HaTorah 2:3-4.*

however, that the soul has a number of parts. Either the entire soul may become a *dybbuk*, or only certain parts of the soul.

Similarly, a soul may be either entirely or partially reincarnated, in which case it is a *Gilgul*. The main difference between a *Gilgul* and a *dybbuk* is that a *Gilgul* has returned to the higher realms and been sent back, while a *dybbuk* has never ascended. Additionally, a *Gilgul* is usually one soul in one body, while a *dybbuk* is multiple souls or parts of souls in one body.

Exorcism

In incredibly rare cases, a *dybbuk* might assert influence upon its host. In these rare instances, the *dybbuk* has been given permission from on high in order that it may be exorcised. It must be understood that a *dybbuk* is neither evil nor demonic. Rather, the process of possession and exorcism is a rare opportunity for the atonement of both the *dybbuk* and the person within whom it resides. The process of exorcism is one of assisting the soul in making *tikkunim*, repairs, and helping it to repent in whatever way possible absent a body. Once this process is completed, the soul is then capable of ascending.

However, this process is only possible with the assistance of another soul, an exalted soul that can invoke the will of *Shamayim*. This would be the soul of a *tsaddik* or scholar who is capable of assisting the *dybbuk*. Without the proximity of such an individual, an exorcism is not possible. Since an exorcism is not possible, there is no point to the possession. Therefore, it won't happen.

There are very specific criteria for determining legitimate cases of possession. These are incredibly exact requirements and preclude any known physiological, psychiatric, or medical cause for the condition.

Since there are no people capable of exorcising a soul nowadays, legitimate cases of possession do not occur. The last verified case was in Lithuania in the 1930's and involved the Chofetz Chaim, Rabbi Yisrael Meir Poupko (Kagan).

Shedim

Any time that you come across the word "demon" in translations of the Talmud or Midrash, it is almost always a translation of the Hebrew term *Sheid*. Like many translations of Hebrew words, though, it is polluted by Christological connotations.

Shedim are odd creatures, having both qualities of men and angels. Although they must eat and drink, they are only loosely bound by the constraints of time and space. Unlike angels, they can manifest physical form, yet only subject to certain conditions.

Additionally, they are bound by their own concept of Torah law, for which they may be held liable and judged in *Bais Din*, Rabbinic Courts. They also live subject to their own strict social order and are subjects of their own king.

In the past, man had frequent interactions with the *Shedim*. Their relationship to man was complicated and involved a lot of confusion and headache. A major problem is that non-Jewish nations constantly took to worshiping the *Shedim* as deities. The Talmud records that the sages made a number of laws limiting their relationship with man. This legislation culminated with the banishment of *Shedim* from all inhabited areas. Nevertheless, certain *halachos*, religious laws, exist that pertain to them. For example:

- One should not enter a house or other property that has been abandoned for 7 years.

- When remodeling a house, one should not completely seal up any of the doors or windows.

- When building an extension onto a home, one has to verify if it involves extending the property over land onto which a drainpipe or gutter opens. If so, then about a foot of dirt on either side, in front of, and beneath the drainpipe opening must be dug and transported to an uninhabited area.

There are a number of other *halachos* related to *Shedim*. However, most of them are not observed anymore due to the rarity of *Shedim*. A noted Kabbalist once told this author that their interaction with people is so rare that it is as if they do not even exist anymore.

Shedim are not singled out as evil or unusual in anyway. They are as much an ordinary part of creation as cows, the sun, spiders, or cats. Like any other animal or person, however, one should not seek to provoke them. The Talmud tells us that if you don't care about them, then they won't care about you.

Summary of This Lesson

1. The sages were not superstitious. They did not assign supernatural causes to phenomena simply because they did not understand its physical causes.

2. A ghost, for lack of a better term, is a disembodied soul. It can be sensed, but has no physical form.

3. Souls and angels have no physical form or existence at all.

4. An apparition is the perception of a disembodied soul by the mind's eye. To intentionally conjure such an apparition is a severe prohibition.

5. Angels are messengers of God that exist to carry out very specific missions. Their names indicate their mission and purpose.

6. Angels have no will independent of God's will. In this sense, they are solely a tool or mechanism used by God.

7. All or part of a soul that has become disembodied and attached to another living person is a *dybbuk*.

8. All or part of soul that has ascended and returned again is a *Gilgul*.

9. Rarely, a *dybbuk* may be allowed to assert itself for the purpose of being exorcised. This is for the benefit of the *dybbuk* and the possessed individual.

10. This only occurs when there is one in proximity who is capable of exorcising the *dybbuk*. The last confirmed case of a full *dybbuk* was over 80 years ago. Since that time there has not been anyone capable of exorcising one.

THE YESHIVA PIRCHEI SHOSHANIM SHULCHAN ARUCH PROJECT

The Noahide Laws – Moshiach Part I

164 Village Path, Lakewood NJ 08701 732.370.3344
164 Rabbi Akiva, Bnei Brak, 03.616.6340

Table of Contents:

The Messiah I

Introduction

The pre-Messianic era, Messianic era, and identity of the Messiah himself are complicated and often misunderstood topics that involve a number of people and a process of unfolding events. While the grand details are known with certainty, specific elements must remain speculation until the actual time comes. In this lesson we will review the facts and questions regarding the coming of the Messiah.

The Pre-Messianic Era

Numerous scriptural prophecies, Midrashim, and other sources tell us that, as the time of the Messiah draws near, the world will experience changes and upheavals. Many of these will be positive, while others will be devastating.

Changes in Religion and Belief

> *Truth will* ne'ederes *[fail]*…
> Isaiah 59:15

The Talmud[1] explains that the word *ne'ederes* is also related to the word for "flocks." The implication of the verse is that truth will fail because the Torah world will be divided into various groups, or flocks, each of which will claim the truth for its own. True Torah and faith will become indistinguishable from that which is false.

Rise of Atheism

Atheism will engulf the world and religious studies will become despised in the era preceding the Messiah.[2] The Jewish world will not be spared from this calamity – many Jews will abandon the Torah and their faith as well. However, the wise will recognize that this torrent of disbelief is a test and that they must remain firm in their faith. This is the interpretation[3] of the verse:

---

[1] Sanhedrin 97a.

[2] *Sichos HaRan* 35.

[3] See Rambam *Iggres Teiman* and *Sichos HaRan* 35 ,220.

Many shall purify themselves — make themselves white and be refined; but the wicked shall do wickedly; and none of the wicked shall understand; but they that are wise shall understand.
Daniel 12:15

There are many who are far from Torah and truth, however, who will see what is happening and realize its import. They will return to God, yet they will suffer ridicule for abandoning the norms of secular culture.   This is the meaning of the verse:

He who departs from evil will be considered a fool.
Isaiah 59:15.

**Social &
National
Upheaval &
Decline**

This decline in religious unity will be, partially, the result of a general global decline in values, morals, and important social institutions.[4] Because change will advance so rapidly, parents and children will experience the world on radically different terms.[5]   As a result, there will be no respect of the elderly or for one's parents. Governments will become godless and economies will fail.[6]

This will all be accompanied by a sudden increase in world population.[7]

This will be a time of tremendous strain. The Midrash states:

One-third of the world's suffering will come in the generation before the Messiah.[8]
According to some recent authorities,[9] there will be an explosion of secular and scientific knowledge before the coming of the Messiah. This is understood from a passage in the Zohar:

**Increase in
Secular
Knowledge**

In the 600th year of the 6th millennium, the supernal gates of wisdom and the lower wellsprings of wisdom will open. This will prepare the world to enter the 7th millennium just as man prepares for Sabbath before sunset.[10]

---

[4] Sotah 49b; Sanhedrin ibid. See also *Shir HaShirim Rabbah* 2:13. Also Zohar 3:67b.

[5] See Kaplan, *Handbook of Jewish Thought* II 24:12.

[6] Sanhedrin 97a – "The son of David will not come until the last penny has gone out from the purse."

[7] *Tosafos* to Niddah 13b s.v. ad *she-yikhlu.*

[8] *Midrash Tehillim* 22:9.

[9] Most notably Rabbi Aryeh Kaplan in a number of his books and essays.

This prophecy establishes the Hebrew year 5600 (1839/1840) as the start of a new era in Human knowledge. Though we cannot tie this Zohar to any specific even in that year, it does correspond to the onset of the scientific revolution and modern technological era.

Ingathering of Exiles

He will gather the dispersed of Israel
Psalms 147:2

God will then bring back your remnants and have mercy on you. God your Lord will once again gather you from among all the nations where He scattered you.
Deuteronomy 30:3

Either after or concurrent with the pre-messianic upheavals there will be a return of the Jewish people to their ancestral land. The unfolding of this process, whether gradual or sudden, miraculous or natural, is uncertain.[11] However it occurs, it will only be completed by the Messiah himself:

On that day, God will stretch forth his hand a second time to recover His people… He will send up a banner for the nations, assemble the dispersed of Israel, and gather together the scattered of Judah from the four corners of the earth.
Isaiah 11:11-12

Restoration of Prophecy

Besides the prophetic indications of a national return, it is also a necessary component of the redemptive process. It appears that the coming of the Messiah is concomitant with a return of prophecy.[12]

---

[10] Zohar I:117a

[11] It is not 100% clear if the current resettlement of Israel constitutes this pre-Messianic ingathering. On one hand, Kesubos 111a discourages the en-masse return to Israel prior to the coming of the Messiah (according to many). However, there are opinions that the return will began with some sort of political independence (see Rabbi Chama in Sanhedrin 98a) and possibly involve the consent and assistance of other nations (Ramban on Song of Songs 8:13, Radak to Psalms 146:3, Abarbanel to Psalms 147:2, and many, many more). Nevertheless, we should pray that the current Jewish resettlement of Israel is this much anticipated messianic prequel.

[12] See Joel 3:1 to 5 and Rambam *Igros Teiman*. Additionally, the Messiah will be king. Kings can only be anointed by a prophet. As well, the Messiah himself will be a prophet (see *Hilchos Teshuva* 9:2)

However, this can only happen when a number of other conditions are fulfilled, one of which is that the majority of the Jewish population must reside in the land of Israel. Therefore, there must be a resettlement prior to the advent of the Messiah.

Cultivation of the Land

O mountains of Israel, let your branches sprout forth and yield your fruit to My people Israel, for they are at hand to come.
Ezekiel 36:8

I will open rivers on the high hills and fountains in the midst of the valleys. I will make the wilderness a pool of water and the dry land springs of water. I will plant in the wilderness cedar, the acacia, myrtle, and the oil-tree. I will set in the desert cypress, the plane-tree, and the larch together so that they may see, and know, and consider, and understand together, that the hand of HaShem has done this, and the Holy One of Israel has created it.
Isaiah 41: 18 - 20[13]

These passages are only a sampling of those prophesying a renewed cultivation of the land of Israel prior to the redemption.[14]

The War of Gog and Magog

One of the final steps in the messianic advent is the War of Gog and Magog. The Book of Ezekiel, chapters 38 and 39, prophecies a war in the era immediately preceding the Messiah. This war, according to the Zohar[15], will take place in the vicinity of Jerusalem. It will be the final showdown for the Land of Israel, a battle royale for the soul of the land. Upon its conclusion, the Jews will live free of harassment in their land.[16] According to Rabbi Akiva[17], the war will last one year.

---

[13] See interpretation of Rabbi Abba, Sanhedrin 98a.

[14] See also Isaiah 49:18 – 22, Jeremiah 33:10-11.

[15] 2:32a.

[16] *Sifrei* Bamidbar 76, Deuteronomy 43. See also Sanhedrin 97b.

[17] Eduyos 2:10.

Though the names of Gog and Magog appear early in Tanakh[18], the exact identities of these nations in modern terms is uncertain. According to the Talmud[19], the second Psalm is a reference to this eventual conflict

The Two Messiahs

It is little known that there actually are two Messiahs: Moshiach ben David (Messiah, son of David) and Moshiach ben Yosef (Messiah, son of Joseph – sometimes called Moshiach ben Ephraim). This is alluded to in numerous places:

And you, son of man, take one stick, and write upon it: For Judah, and for the children of Israel his companions; then take another stick, and write upon it: For Joseph, the stick of Ephraim, and of all the house of Israel his companions; and join them one to another into one stick, that they may become one in your hand.
Ezekiel 37:16-17

Ephraim's envy will depart and Judah's enemies will be cut off. Ephraim will not envy Judah and Judah will not envy nor harass Ephraim.
Isaiah 11:13

Of particular importance is the latter verse teaching that each of the Messiahs will have their own missions uniquely suited to their strengths. They will not envy one another nor interfere with their respective jobs. Each Messiah will have his own era, as well, with the Era of Moshiach ben Yosef coming first.[20]

Moshiach Ben Yosef

All messianic tasks up to and including the War of Gog and Magog will be the duties of Moshiach ben Yosef. It is he who will wage the war and conquer:

The house of Jacob shall be a fire, and the house of Joseph a flame, and the house of Esau stubble. They will set them ablaze and consume them; there will be no survivor of the house of Esau, for God has spoken.
Obadiah 1:18

---

[18] I.e. Genesis 10:2.

[19] Avodah Zara 3b.

[20] There is some disagreement about the exact order of these two eras. *Tosafos* Eruvin43b presents an argument that ben Yosef must precede ben David. However, Rashi *ad loc.* disagrees. Most scholars agree with Tosafos. There is a tremendous amount written on this subject..

It appears that this Messiah will die in battle, though, and be mourned by Israel:

They shall look to Me because they have pushed him through, and they shall mourn for him as one mourns for a first born son.
Zechariah 12:10

According to some scholars, however, the decree of death for Moshiach ben Yosef was rescinded. [21]

Eliyahu HaNavi

Following the War of Gog and Magog[22], the prophet Elijah will herald the impending messianic age:

Behold! I will send Elijah the Prophet before the coming of the great and awesome day of God! He will turn the hearts of the fathers to their children and of the children to their fathers…
Malachi 3:23

As we see in the verse, he will turn people back to truth and rectify much of the world's pre-messianic decline. Immediately following his arrival, the final Messiah, ben David, will be revealed. [23]

In the second part of this lesson, we will examine the qualifications and duties of Moshiach ben David.

---

[21] See *Kol HaTor* 1:6 and 8. The Ari Z"l also says that the death of ben Yosef is not an absolute certainty.

[22] *Emunos VeDeyos* 8:2.. Some, however, maintain that Eliyahu will come before the war.

[23] Eruvin 43b and *Tos. Ad loc.* See also Rash on Eduyos 8:7, *Hilchos Nazirus* 4:11.

Summary of This Lesson

1. There are a number of stages to the coming of the Messiah.

2. The first is a period of social, spiritual, and political decline.

3. According to contemporary understandings of the Zohar, there will be an explosion of secular wisdom concurrent with these travails.

4. There will be tremendous difficulty discerning truth from falsehood in these times. The wise will see and recognize the greater significance of these events.

5. Concurrent with or following this era will be a return of the Jews to their ancestral land. This return is an intrinsic part of the eventual return of prophecy.

6. The land will be cultivated and bloom again.

7. As the population increases and the former glory is Israel approaches its return, there will be a Great War: the War of Gog and Magog.

8. This war will be waged on behalf of God by Moshiach ben Yosef, one of the two Messiahs.

9. Either immediately before or after this war (after, according to most) Elijah the prophet will appear to announce and make final preparations for the final Messiah, Moshiach ben David.

The Noahide Laws – Moshiach Part II

Table of Contents:

The Messiah II

Introduction

In our previous lesson we examined the events of the pre-messianic era and the coming of *Moshiach ben Yosef* (Messiah son of Joseph). *Moshiach ben Yosef*, however, is only one of two messiahs. The second, final messiah is *Moshiach ben David*, the Davidic messiah. When most people speak of the messiah, they are referring to this final messianic figure. In this lesson we will examine the criteria for identifying the messiah, his duties, and the messianic age.

Criteria for the Davidic Messiah

The Torah belief[1] is that the final Messiah, *Moshiach ben Dovid*, will be identified by six criteria:

1) He will be a direct descendant of King David,
2) He will be anointed as king of Israel,
3) He will complete the return of the Jewish people to Israel,
4) He will rebuild the temple in Jerusalem,
5) He will bring peace to the world, ending all war,
6) He will bring knowledge of God to the world.

These six criteria are not metaphorical – they are literal, observable, verifiable facts. They are the minimum that one must accomplish before he is accepted as the Messiah.

---

[1] Hilchos Melachim 11:1.

Writes the Rambam[2]:

If there arises a ruler from the family of David, immersed in the Torah and its mitzvos as was his ancestor David, who observes both the Oral and Written Torahs, who leads Israel back to the Torah, strengthening its observance and waging God's battles, then we may presume that he is the Messiah. If he then succeeds in rebuilding the temple upon its original site and gathering in the exiles of Israel, his identity as Messiah will then be confirmed.

Once a candidate meets criteria 1, 2, 5 and 6, we may presume he is the messiah. Once he completes stages 3 and 4, he is confirmed as the messiah. Our sages teach us to nevertheless remain skeptical of messianic claims:

Said Rabbi Yochanan ben Zakkai: If you are holding a sapling in your hand and someone tells you, 'Come quickly, the messiah is here!', first finish planting the tree and then go to greet the messiah.[3]

When Will the Messiah Arrive?

The messiah can come at any time and will arrive (reveal himself) on any day except a Shabbat or a Holiday.[4]

However, we should never try to calculate or predict the time of the arrival of the messiah. The sages curse[5] those who attempt to predict the dates and times of his arrival because doing so ultimately damages the faith of others:

Rabbi Shmuel ben Nachmani said in the name of Rabbi Yonatan, "The bones of those who calculate the end should rot! For they would say that since the predetermined time has arrived and yet he has not come, he will never come. Rather wait for him, as it is written, 'Even though he might delay, wait for him'[6]

Furthermore, studying, fixating, or obsessing on the messiah as a goal of one's religious thought and practice is discouraged:

---

[2] *Hilchos Melachim* 11:4.

[3] Avos 31b.

[4] Eruvin 43a.

[5] Sanhedrin 97a.

[6] Isaiah 30:18

A person should not involve himself with the Aggadot [Talmudic sections regarding Mashiach] nor with the words of the Midrash that speak about this topic. Do not make them the prime focus, because they do not bring a person to love or fear of God. Also do not calculate the end [time of Mashiach's arrival] ... Rather wait for him and believe in the general principle, as we have explained.[7]

The goal of our study and service of God should be to fulfill His will in this world at every moment. Focusing on the future redemption only diminishes one's *Avodah* (divine service) in the here-and-now.

1. A Descendant of David

A shoot will come forth from the family of Jesse and a branch will grow from his roots
Isaiah 11:1

This is one of many verses indicating that the messiah will arise from the family of David.[8] As mentioned, this is not a metaphor – he will actually be able to trace his lineage definitively to King David. There are many, many Jewish families today who can trace their ancestry to King David. Many of them are descendants of the Maharal, Rabbi Yehudah Loewy (1512 to 1609). Rabbi Loewy was a descendant of King David via his *Geonic* ancestry.

Jewish Ancestry

I see him, but not now; I behold him, but not nigh; there shall step forth a star <u>out of Jacob,</u> and a scepter shall rise **out of Israel,** *and shall smite through the corners of Moab, and break down all the sons of Seth.*
Numbers 24:17

When you come into the land which the Lord your God gave you, and shall possess it, and dwell within it, and say: 'I will set a king over me like all the nations that are around about me,' then you will set over you as king a wise man whom the Lord your G-d shall choose. You shall set one from among your brethren_as king over you. You may not place a stranger over you who is not your brother.
Deuteronomy 17:14-15

---

[7] *Hilchos Melachim* 12:2.

[8] See the commentaries of Ibn Ezra and Radak to Isaiah. See also Sanhedrin 98a and *Eikhah Rabbah* 1:51.

These two versus inform us that the messiah must be Jewish. Since the messiah will also be anointed as a King of Israel, he must be Jewish. Jewish is defined as born of a Jewish mother.[9]

From the Tribe of Judah

*The scepter shall not depart **from Judah** nor the ruler's staff from between his feet as long as men come to Shiloh; and unto him shall the obedience of the peoples be.* Genesis 49:10.

The messiah must come from the tribe of Judah. Tribal affiliation is only passed through the father's lineage.[10]

2. A King of Israel

The term *Moshiach*, messiah, literally means "anointed with oil." Throughout the Tanakh there are many individuals who are called *Moshiach* on account of being anointed. Anointing with oil at the hands of a prophet was one of the many requirements for Jewish kingship. For example, the prophet Samuel anointed both Kings Saul and David with oil.[11]

Since the messiah will be crowned king, he must be anointed by a prophet. This is one of the reasons for the prophet Malachi's prophesy that Elijah would return prior to the messiah.[12]

3. Return of the Jewish People to Israel

He will arise a banner for the nations and assemble the castaways of Israel; and He will gather in the dispersed ones of Judah from the four corners of the earth.
Isaiah 11:12

It shall be on that day that Hashem will thresh, from the surging [Euphrates] River to the Brook of Egypt, and you [Israel] will be gathered up one by one, O Children of Israel. It shall be on that day that a great shofar will be blown, and those who are lost in the land of Assyria and those cast away in the land of Egypt will come [together], and they will prostrate themselves to Hashem on the holy mountain in Jerusalem.

---

[9] See Lev. 24:10 and Ezra 10:2-3. Kiddush 68.

[10] See Numbers 34:14, Numbers 1:18-44, Leviticus 24:10.

[11] See I Samuel 15:1, 16:1 to 13.

[12] Malachi 3:23-24.

Isaiah 27:12-13

I will return the captivity of Judah and captivity of Israel, and will rebuild them as at first.
Jeremiah 33:7

The return of the Jewish people to the land is not only part of the restoration of
the glory of Israel, but is necessary for the return of prophecy. As we saw in the
previous lesson, the Messiah will be the greatest prophet ever, second only to
Moses.[13] As it is written:

*He will be filled with the spirit of God; he will not judge by what his eyes see or decide by what
his ears hear.*
Isaiah 11:13.

Among the many requirements for prophecy is that the majority of the Jewish
people live in the land of Israel. [14]

**Restoration of
Tribal Identities**
Using his power of prophecy, the messiah will clarify the tribal identities of the
Jewish people. In particular, he will determine the legitimacy of the *Kohanim* and
Leviim.[15] He will then divide the land according to the ancestral heritage of each.

4. Rebuilding of the Temple

*I will seal a covenant of peace with them; it will be an eternal covenant with them; and I
will emplace them and increase them, and I will place My Sanctuary among them
forever. My dwelling place will be among them; I will be a God to them and they will be
a people to Me. Then the nations will know that I am Hashem who sanctifies Israel,
when My Sanctuary will be among them forever.*
Ezekiel 37:26-28

---

[13] *Hilchos Teshuva* 9:2.

[14] See Yoma 9b, Sanhedrin 11a, Brachos 57a, Sukkah 28a, Bava Basra 134a and many, many others.

[15] See Malachi 3:3.

It will be in the end of days that the Mountain of the Temple of Hashem will be firmly established as the most prominent of the mountains, and it will be exalted up above the hills, and peoples will stream to it.
Micah 4:1

It will happen in the end of days; The Mountain of the Temple of Hashem will be firmly established as the head of the mountains, and it will be exalted above the hills, and all the nations will stream to it. Many peoples will go and say, 'Come, let us go up to the Mountain of Hashem, to the Temple of the God of Jacob, and He will teach us of His ways and we will walk in His paths.
Isaiah 2: 2, 3

The Messiah will accomplish the rebuilding of the Third temple according to the details prophesied by Ezekiel.[16]   According to many,[17] this is the act which definitively proves the identity of the messiah.

Many details of the rebuilding, such as the precise location of the altar, must be determined using prophecy.[18] For this reason, we know that the messiah must have prophecy. This also means that rebuilding the temple prior to the advent of the messiah is impossible.

Reestablishment of the Sanhedrin

The Messiah will also reestablish the Sanhedrin, which is a precursor to the re-establishment of the Temple:

I will restore your judges as at first, your counselors as in the beginning. Afterwards you will be called the city of righteousness, the faithful city. Zion shall be redeemed with justice…
Isaiah 1:26-27.

At some point between the coming of Elijah and the reestablishment of the Sanhedrin, formal *Semicha* (rabbinic ordination) will be restored. This is necessary for one to serve on the Sanhedrin. The chain of ordination from Moses was broken by Roman oppression in 358 CE. The possibility of renewing this ordination and reconstituting the Sanhedrin prior to the Messiah has been raised in the past, in particularly by Rabbi Yaakov Beirav in Tsfas in the 16th century.

---

[16] Chapters 40 to 48.

[17] *Hilchos Melachim* 11:4.

[18] *Zevachim* 62a. When Ezra rebuilt the temple only a few decades after its destruction, prophecy was required to locate the place of the altar.   So too it will be needed to rebuild the final temple.

However, the attempt failed upon the ruling of the Radbaz, Rabbi Dovid ben Zimra, that the establishment of Semicha was not possible in our times.

The Temple Service

The messiah will also restore the sacrificial system to whatever degree it will apply in the Messianic era. He will also reestablish the Sabbatical and Jubilee year observances.

5. Establishing Peace and the End of All Wars

I will seal a covenant of peace with them; it will be an eternal covenant with them; and I will emplace them and increase them, and I will place My Sanctuary among them forever.
Ezekiel 37:26

He will judge between many peoples, and will settle the arguments of mighty nations from far away. They will beat their swords into plowshares and their spears into pruning knives; nation will not lift sword against nations, nor will they learn war anymore.
Micah 4:3

He will judge among the nations, and will settle the arguments of many peoples. They shall beat their swords into plowshares and their spears into pruning hooks; nation will not lift sword against nation and they will no longer study warfare.
Isaiah 2:4

The Messiah will be a great political leader who will make peace among the nations. All war will come to an end and the nations will work for the mutual benefit of the world.

6. He Will Bring Awareness of God

They will neither injure nor destroy in all of My sacred mountain; for the earth will be as filled with knowledge of Hashem as water covering the sea bed.
Isaiah 11:9

The glory of Hashem will be revealed, and all flesh together will see that the mouth of Hashem has spoken.
Isaiah 40:5

For then I will change the nations [to speak] a pure language, so that they all will proclaim the
Name of Hashem, to worship Him with a united resolve.
Zephaniah 3:9

They will no longer teach - each man his fellow, each man his brother-saying, "Know Hashem!
For all of them will know Me, from their smallest to their greatest - the word of Hashem - when
I will forgive their iniquity and will no longer recall their sin.
Jeremiah   31:33

The most important mission of the Messiah will be to bring awareness of God to the world. Under his leadership all mankind will effortlessly achieve the highest levels of divine inspiration.

Free Will

Man will still have free will at this time and the potential to do evil will still exist. However, the awareness of God will be so intense and immediately apparent that there will be no incentive to do evil.[19] Instead man will endeavor only to understand God and his Torah.

Conversion

As the messiah approaches, many non-Jews will rush to convert to Judaism.[20] Once the Messiah ben David is revealed, however, converts will not be accepted anymore.[21]

The Messiah's End

The Messiah will be a human being like any other.[22] He will have human parents and, like all men, will die a human death.[23] However, his reign will last for a very, very long time because lifespans in *Olam HaBa* (the messianic world) will be greatly extended.

---

[19] Sotah 52a; Zohar I:109a; See also Ramchal *Maamar Ikkarim.*

[20] See Zephania 3:9; Avodah Zarah 24a; Berachos 57b.

[21] Avodah Zarah 3b and *Maharal Chiddushei Aggados* ad loc.

[22] *Hilchos Melachim* 11:3.

[23] See Rambam to Sanhedrin 10:1.

Summary

- There are six criteria that one must fulfill in order to be the messiah:

  1. He will be a direct descendant of King David,
  2. He will be anointed as king of Israel,
  3. He will complete the return of the Jewish people to Israel,
  4. He will rebuild the temple in Jerusalem,
  5. He will bring peace to the world, ending all war,
  6. He will bring knowledge of God to the world.

- The Messiah will be human, born of human parents, and will die a human death.

- Calculating the time at which he will arrive is forbidden and those who do so are cursed.

- While the messiah is a tenet of Torah faith, it should not be overly emphasized. Our duty is to fulfill Gods will in the here and now.

The Noahide Laws – Prophecy and Inspiration

Table of Contents:

Prophecy & Inspiration

Introduction

The Tanach is replete with examples of divine inspiration, whether mere assistance or outright prophecy. What is prophecy? Does it exist today? How does God speak to us? In this lesson we are going to provide an overview of divine assistance, inspiration, and prophecy.

Siyata D'Shmaya - Divine Assistance

The lowest level of inspiration is what we can best call "divine assistance.[1]" Though not uncommon, it is so that those who have it are usually unaware of it.[2] This level of inspiration is given to all of those who teach Torah in public with the proper motivations and fear of God.[3] This level of inspirations is alluded to in many places. For example in Psalms 25:14:

The counsel of HaShem is with them that fear Him; and His covenant, to make them know it.

This was the minimal level of inspiration possessed by all leaders in the Tanach and Talmud. Any Torah leader whose works have been accepted by all or a substantial portion of Israel is assumed to have possessed this level of inspiration. This level can be attained by any person in any time or place.

Ruach HaKodesh – Divine Inspiration

Ruach HaKodesh is the next highest level of inspiration. At this level a person is aware that God is guiding his actions.[4] However, it is still not prophecy.

---

[1] Moreh Nevuchim II:45.

[2] Kuzari II:14, III:32, and III:65

[3] Shir HaShirim Rabbah 1:8 – 9.

[4] See Ramban to Shemos 28:30 and Derech HaShem III:3:1 – 3.

Prophecy, as we shall see, is a communication between God and man. *Ruach HaKodesh* is not communication. Rather, it is inspiration and guidance. Through it a person develops unique intuition as to future events[5] and even the thoughts and actions of others.[6] There are ten qualities a person must perfect before he is even minimally worthy of this inspiration:[7]

- **Torah** – he must be unceasingly involved in the study and teaching of Torah.

- *Zehirus*, caution - He must be extremely careful to never violate a negative commandment.

- *Zerizus*, zeal – he must zealously perform every positive commandment.

- **Nekius,** cleanliness – he must be clean of sin in thought and desire.

- **Perishus,** abstention – he must sanctify himself even in that which is permitted and abstain from it if it may possibly lead to untoward desires or actions.

- **Tahara,** purity – he must have repented and cleanse himself of all sin, having righted all his past wrongs.

- **Chasidus**, piety – complete dedication to God beyond the letter of the law, but in the spirit of the law as well.

- **Anavah,** humility – complete nullification of ego and self.

- **Yiras Chet** – Dread and fear of sin.

- **Kedusha,** holiness – separation from worldly needs and desires.

Once these qualities have been mastered, then the initiate may engage in meditations, certain rituals, or methods of intense Torah study in order to merit *Ruach ha-kodesh.*

---

[5] R' Bachya to Lev. 8:8 and Derech HaShem ibid.

[6] Eliahu Rabbah to OC 101:8. See also Maharitz Chayes to Shabbos 12b.

[7] See Avodah Zarah 20b. Mishnayos Sotah 9:14.

Within this level there are many gradations that may be attained in greater or lesser measure.

The *Ketuvim*, Writings, were written in a state of *Ruach haKodesh*, divine inspiration, while the Prophets were written in a state of *Nevuah*, prophecy. That is why the Prophets are on a higher level than the writings. [8]

Nevuah - Prophecy

At first, prophecy was attainable by all human beings. Moses, however, prayed that it be granted to Israel alone – a request to which God agreed:

And he [Moses] said unto Him: 'If Your presence go not with me, carry us not up. For wherein now shall it be known that I have found grace in Your sight - I and Thy people? Is it not in that you go with us, so that we are distinguished, I and Thy people, from all the people that are upon the face of the earth?' And HaShem said unto Moses: 'I will do this thing that you have spoken, for you have found grace in My sight, and I know you by name.' [9]

This restriction went into effect upon completion of the tabernacle.[10] From that moment on, prophecy was not granted to non-Jews unless it was for the sake of Israel.[11] Even in these instances, however, the prophetic vision was the bare minimum needed to convey the message. It would come secretly, at night, and in a vague form. This is the statement of the prophet:

Now a word was brought to me secretly.[12]

---

[8] Moreh Nevukhim II:45. There are numerous, vast discussions about the relative holiness of these books.

[9] Exodus 33:16-17; see Brachos 7b and Bava Basra 15b for explanation and interpretation.

[10] Vayikra Rabbah I:12 and Shir HaShirim Rabbah II:12.

[11] See the previous footnote for sources.

[12] Job 4:12.

CONDITIONS FOR PROPHECY

Even with the restriction of prophecy to Israel alone, a number of conditions must exist for prophecy to take place:

Land of Israel and Her People

Prophecy is only possible in the land of Israel when the majority of the Jewish people are living there:

> *HaShem, your G-d, with raise up a prophet for your,* **from your midst, from your brethren,** *like me. To him shall you listen.*[13]

The bold section indicates that prophecy is only possible in Israel when it is inhabited by the Jewish people. This is because prophecy requires a particular degree of *Kedushah*, holiness, which is only possible in Israel and in the midst of the people of Israel.[14]

Once a prophet has mastered prophecy in Israel, he can then attain prophecy even outside of Israel.[15] However this prophecy will be harder to achieve and only granted in specific circumstances.[16]

The Ark of the Covenant

Full prophecy is only possible when the Ark of the Covenant rests in the temple. At that time, the influence of the Ark, the root of prophecy in this world, extended to the boundaries of the land of Israel.[17]

Worthiness of the individual

There are a number of qualities a person must possess as a prerequisite to prophecy:

- Must be of pure Israelite lineage[18] and a direct descendant of Abraham.[19] Moses alluded to this when he said:

---

[13] Deuteronomy 18:15.

[14] Sifrei; Yalkut Shimoni I:919.

[15] See commentaries to Ezekiel 1:3.

[16] Kuzari II:14; Maharitz Chayes to Moed Katan 25a; Mekhilta to exodus 12:1.

[17] Sefer Ikkarim III:11.

*God, your Lord, will elevate a prophet from you... **from your brethren, just like me**[20]* - meaning of Israelite ancestry like Moses himself[21]

- o This is a general rule, however. Exceptions have been made for those of special merit, such as Obadiah.[22]

- A potential prophet must possess a number of personal qualities as pre-requisites:[23]

  - o Must be mentally healthy and stable[24]
  - o Must have a mature intellect which has maximized its potential[25]
  - o Must be an expert in all areas of the Torah.[26]
  - o Must have what he needs and be materially completely satisfied with no desires materially for more or less.[27]

- The generation must be capable of meriting prophecy. Prophecy is only granted for the sake of God's people.[28] Even if an individual is worthy and

---

[18] See Kiddushin 70b & Tos. Ad loc. See also Yevamos 47b and Niddah 13b. See also Kuzari I:114.

[19] See Bamidbar Rabbah 12:4; Rashi to Sanhedrin 39b.

[20] Deuteronomy 18:15

[21] Sifrei, Yalkut Shimoni I:919. See also Rashi there and Rambam in the Iggeros Teiman.

[22] See Sanhedrin 39b.

[23] Shabbat 92a and Nedarim 38a.

[24] Moreh Nevukhim II:36.

[25] Moreh Nevukhim Ibid; Nedarim 38a; Hil. Yesodei HaTorah 7:1.

[26] See Shu"t HaRashba 548.

[27] Moreh Nevukhim ibid.; Avos 4:1; Shemonah Perkim 7.

[28] Mekhilta Shemos 12:1. See also Rashi to Devarim 2:16 and Shelah to Taanis II:137a.

capable of receiving prophecy, it will not be bestowed if the Generation is not worthy or capable of recognizing true prophecy.[29]

Once these minimum benchmarks are met, the candidate may begin to prepare for prophecy. This involves techniques of meditation and focus to attain the state required for prophecy.[30]

Master & Guide

Every potential prophet must have a master to guide him and constantly give him "reality checks."[31] Without a master to teach him and keep him on the right track, the result of his efforts will be psychosis and hallucinations.[32]

The Experience of Prophecy

Prophecy, being a skill and a craft, is something the prophet works to perfect over a long period of time.[33] His first early prophecies will be flawed, unfocused and possibly unrecognizable as prophecy.[34]

As his prophecy is perfected, it may be experienced as either a waking vision or a nocturnal dream:[35]

> *And He said: 'Hear now My words: if there be a prophet among you, I HaShem will make Myself known unto him in a vision, I will speak with him in a dream.[36]*

The type of prophetic experience indicates greater and lesser degrees of prophetic ability. In ascending order of ability:

- A Waking vision is always higher than a dream vision.

---

[29] Sanhedrin 11a; Brachos 57a; Succos 28a; Bava Basra 134a.

[30] See Hil. Yesodei HaTorah 7:4. These techniques are discussed in a number of sources.

[31] See Derech HaShem III:4:4.

[32] See Maharsha to Shabbat 149b and Sanhedrin 89a. See also Derech HaShem III:4:6.

[33] Derech HaShem Ibid.

[34] Derech HaShem Ibid.

[35] Pirkei R' Eliezer 28. Yesodei HaTorah 7:2. Derech HaShem III:5:2.

[36] Numbers 12:6.

- Hearing words is higher than seeing visions.
- Seeing the speaker of the words is higher than only hearing them.
- Seeing an angelic speaker is higher than seeing a human speaker.

The prophetic experience cannot be had if the prophet is depressed or angry.[37] He must be in a pleasant, content, happy mood in order to enter the prophetic state.[38] For this reason, we often see music connected to the prophetic experience.[39]

According to many, the voice one hears in a prophecy is the Prophet's own.[40] The face he may see is his own as well.[41]

PUBLIC PROPHECY

Most of a prophet's visions are private and meant only for the prophet himself.[42] However, a prophet is sometimes sent with a message for others. In such a case, the prophet is forced to reveal it even against his will:

And if I say: 'I will not make mention of Him, nor speak any more in His name', then there is in my heart as it were a burning fire shut up in my bones, and I weary myself to hold it in, but cannot.[43]

Not all public prophecies were recorded and canonized. Only those prophecies that apply to all of Israel at all times were recorded as part of Tanakh.[44]

---

[37] Shabbat 30a; Pesachim 66b and 117a.

[38] Yerushalmi Sukkah 5:1; Bereshis Rabbah 70:8. See also Tos. Sukkos 50b.

[39] I Samuel 10:5; II Kings 3:15; I Chronicles 25:1. Yesodei HaTorah 7:4.

[40] Shoshon Sodoth. See Brachos 45a that God spoke to Moses with the Voice of Moses.

[41] Shoshan Sodoth.

[42] Derech HaShem III:4:6.

[43] Jeremiah 20:9.

[44] Megillah 14a.

THE PROPHECY OF MOSES

None of the aforementioned applies to Moses. Moses's prophecy was of an entirely different type than all other prophets.[45] Moses spoke to God as one speaks to his fellow, face to face.[46] His prophecy was not in the form of symbols, visions, or dreams, but as a waking, absolutely normal experience. Moreover, Moses was able to engage in direct conversation with God at any time.[47]

PROPHECY'S END

Prophecy was very common during the first temple era. Many times there were over 1,000,000 people who had prophecy.[48]

The period of Prophecy lasted from about 1313 BCE until about 40 years after the building of the second temple (about 313 BCE). Prophecy had begun to wane when the majority of the Jewish people refused to return to Israel with Ezra.[49] Additionally, the Ark was displaced after the destruction of the first temple, which weakened the potential of prophecy. Sadly, there is no prophecy in our times.

---

[45] Bereshis Rabbah 76:1; Zohar I:171a; Hil. Yesodei HaTorah 7:6.

[46] Exodus 33:11.

[47] See Numbers 12:6-8.

[48] Megillah 14a. See also Shir HaShirim Rabbah 4:22 and Ruth Rabbah 1:2.

[49] Yoma 9b.

Summary

- There are three types of heavenly inspiration that exist. Each has its own numerous gradations and subdivision.

- The lowest level is Divine Assistance, and this granted to all those who teach Torah in public for the right reasons. All may attain this.

- The second level is Divine Inspiration. It is rarer than the first type. There are a number of personal qualities that the initiate must possess. This is a form of divine guidance granting the holder unique insight and intuition.

- The highest level is *Nevuah – prophecy*. This is an experience of communication with God via a vision or dream. Prophecy does not exist anymore in our days.